A MARKETING BRAINSTORM

A MARKETING BRAINSTORM

THE THOUGHT PROCESS BEHIND EFFECTIVE MESSAGING, BRANDING, AND AUDIENCES

NIMROD GANZARSKI

Nimrod Ganzarski
A Marketing Brainstorm
The Thought Process behind Effective Messaging, Branding, and Audiences

Published by Spines
ISBN 979-8-89569-937-9

CONTENTS

I wouldn't be marketing if it were not for:

My kids and wife, my parents, siblings, and family.
My neighborhood and friends.
My school and teachers.
Myself, my imaginary friends, my dreams, my fears, my anxiety, and my optimism.
The people I don't know now, but will soon.

Thank you all.

SECTION 1: FOUNDATIONS OF MARKETING AND AUDIENCE UNDERSTANDING

1

MARKETING IS EASY. PREPARING FOR IT IS NOT

I'd like to introduce you to the rectangle of marketing as I have learned to understand it after more than 25 years in a changing, weird, frightening, fun, and educating market. It doesn't matter if it's B2C, B2B, B2B2C, or any other combination; the basics are the same everywhere:

The Rectangle of Marketing

1. **Who is the Audience?**
2. **What is Their Problem?**
3. **What is Your Solution?**
4. **What Do You Want Them to Do?**

These steps are where creativity and experience truly come into play. Everything else—whether before, during, or after these steps—is technical and can be handled by anyone. The real magic happens in these four stages.

Understanding your audience is the cornerstone of effective marketing. This goes beyond basic demographics, and dives into the psychographics of your target market. It's about understanding their behaviors, needs, and pain points. As David Ogilvy (the "Father of Advertising") once said, "The consumer isn't a moron; she's your wife." This comes to tell you the importance of understanding your audience on a deeper, more personal level.

When Nike targets young athletes, they don't just focus on selling shoes. They sell the aspiration of greatness, the dream of becoming the next Michael Jordan or Serena Williams. They go beyond selling a shoe by understanding the motivations and dreams of their audience and tailoring their messaging to fit that dream (that many have, but still, a dream).

This approach dives deeper than just the "pain point" we've been taught in marketing school. It's about dissecting the "pain point" and understanding its true nature. Simon Sinek once said, "People don't buy what you do; they buy WHY you do it." Understanding the 'why' behind your audience's problem helps in building a message that resonates.

Consider the success of Dollar Shave Club. They identified a common problem many men had but thought there was no solution to - expensive shaving products. So, they offered a simple, affordable, and convenient solution. Their marketing strategy was built around addressing this problem, leading to their rapid growth and eventual acquisition by Unilever. Through extensive research and conversations with many men, they discovered that the problem was not related to the product itself. Many men did not care or see any difference between the brands being sold; they only cared about the buying process and the price.

Your solution must clearly address the identified problem. It's about aligning your product or service with the needs of your audience. As Seth Godin said, "Don't find customers for your products; find products for your customers." This customer-centric approach ensures that your solution is relevant and valuable.

Take Apple's approach, for example. When they launched the iPhone, it wasn't just another phone. It was a revolutionary device that addressed multiple problems—communication, entertainment, and internet browsing—in one designed package. Their solution was innovative, user-friendly, and met the needs of a wide audience.

Creating a memorable brand is an art. It's about crafting a message that sticks and resonates long after the initial interaction. This is where creativity shines. Whether it's through compelling storytelling, innovative advertising, or engaging digital campaigns, the goal is to leave a lasting impression. When you leave that type of impression, your audience will listen ("if you build it, they will come").

Yes, researching your audience is a creative task. Knowing what questions to ask, what your audience answered, and what they HAVE NOT answered... requires creativity. Crafting a memorable message is the visible outcome of this creativity, be it texts, TV ads, digital campaigns, or even street events.

While the steps of marketing are easy to understand, preparing for them is the hard part. It requires creativity, experience, and a deep understanding of your audience. By focusing on these four steps, you can create a marketing strategy that not only reaches your audience but also stays with them.

2

RIGHT MESSAGES, CORRECT AUDIENCES, AND DATA

Think of your message as an arrow.

When you want to deliver your message—whether it's a startup pitch, a sales presentation, or even a policy change within your company—think of your message as an arrow. Literally, write down what you want the other side to take away in one sentence. Now, build the story around it.

You need to know your audience, and once you understand them, take that sentence and craft a single, direct, clear message in simple terms.

Strange as it may sound, your goal isn't to *sell* but to communicate your message. What's the message? That's another story and way of thinking, but before the message starts working, you need to deliver it and ensure your audience understands.

Take presentations, for example.

I'm not suggesting you create a presentation with an all-white background or use fonts and colors in a uniform way. You can design something stunning and colorful while ensuring your message gets across clearly.

Here are some presentation pitfalls that can hurt your message delivery because subconsciously (or consciously), they distract us from the message:

- ❌ Grammatical errors.
- ❌ Spelling mistakes.
- ❌ Design that makes it hard to read the words.
- ❌ Overly innovative and groundbreaking design ideas.
- ❌ Designs that draw attention away from the message.

These and other distractions cause your audience's minds to focus on them rather than on the message. If someone is yelling at us on the street, we won't hear what they're yelling about; we just notice that they're yelling.

Again, your message needs to be consistent and clear, but that doesn't mean plain black text on a white background.

Here's another tip: think about the level of understanding you need from your audience. You can't wrap a tax benefits message in too much humor because then your audience will focus on the humor and not on the benefits or the actions required. The more complex the message is, the cleaner and simpler the wrapping should be.

How does data play into this?

Using data enhances your efforts on multiple levels.

1. **Audience Analysis and Understanding:** Data helps you understand your audience's behavior, language, and the subtle nuances that let you get inside their heads.
2. **Where Is Your Audience?** Where do they consume content? Where do they seek purchase recommendations? Only through data can you start creating the right verticals per media platform. Data also helps you understand what else is in that vertical so you can create content that's similar (or different) from what's already there.
3. **Develop Precise Content:** With the right data, you can understand what kind of content resonates with your audience across different media. What formats? Which genres? And more.
4. **Real-Time Optimization:** By tracking activities in real-time, the digital world allows you to make immediate tweaks and changes to your messages.
5. **Measuring Impact:** If a tree falls in the forest and no one hears it... it's the same with activity and

measurement. Whatever you do, if you don't measure, you'll never be able to advance, improve, and fine-tune your approach to your audience.

To recap: Every communication effort should contain only one message, tailored to the audience, to the media where the message is delivered, and to the level of understanding you need from your audience.

3

THINGS I WISH I'D BEEN TOLD EARLY ON ABOUT AUDIENCES

Honestly, the theory of marketing is easy to understand and plan. The reality, however, hits like a Jackie Chan kick to the face.

On paper, a marketing plan looks neat: define your target audience, build your messages, and launch a campaign, right? But in reality, marketing is a dynamic and complex process where assumptions are often proven wrong left and right. What becomes critical in marketing is not the plan or the execution, but the reaction—especially when theory doesn't align with reality.

I've always wanted to write, "If only someone had told me this when I was starting out..." Well, here I am, writing it now.

I still remember the joy of my first successful marketing move early in my career. But what sticks with me even more is the guilt, the sense of failure, and the self-doubt after my first failure. To be honest, it didn't stop at the first failure. There were many after that. So, let's talk about defining target audiences—because that's one of the trickiest parts of marketing. Why? Because it seems so simple, but it's not. I'll share some early-warning tips and action items for correction.

"Your World Is as Narrow as an Ant's"

Let's start with a recurring issue: defining the target audience based on what you know.

You work in an advertising agency, or on the client side, and you live in the social media world, walking the streets, familiar with your environment. So when you try to define a target audience—it feels easy because it's what you know! Well, that's where you're wrong.

You, your family, your friends, your social media feed, and your neighborhood—they are not your audience. Whether it's a national insurance service or a can of beer—your target audience doesn't live in your world, especially if the product or service isn't relevant to you.

Researching target audiences is crucial for the success of a campaign and the entire sales funnel. Without deep audience research that includes competitor analysis, surveys, interviews, observation, reading, building complex personas, and more, you'll either throw money away or miss out on greater potential revenue. Take this advice seriously: audience research is critical, and it requires time, creativity, and resources to get it right.

By the way, there are two common pitfalls: either missing

who your real audience is or, if you do get the audience right, misunderstanding them.

"A Step Away from Success"

Even big, well-equipped brands can fail in defining or understanding their target audiences. Here are a few examples of misreading the audience or choosing the wrong one:

Pepsi's 2017 Kendall Jenner Ad: Pepsi aired an ad during the height of the Black Lives Matter movement that featured Kendall Jenner handing a Pepsi to a police officer during a protest. The brand tried to appeal to young, socially conscious consumers by suggesting that youth can make a positive, happy change through protest. But the ad backfired. Pepsi was accused of trivializing the BLM movement, showing how a brand's values must align with its audience's—especially on sensitive social issues.

American Airlines' AAirpass Program: In the 1980s, American Airlines introduced a program offering unlimited flights for a one-time fee of $250,000. While they targeted wealthy frequent flyers, they failed to fully understand their audience. Those "wealthy travelers" used the pass much more than expected, resulting in hundreds of flights per year per customer, which cost American Airlines millions in losses.

Mazda Bongo Friendee: In the late 90s, Mazda marketed

this model to young Americans with an adventurous, music-filled campaign. But instead, the car appealed to older, more conservative drivers who valued its simplicity and functionality. Here, Mazda missed the mark in identifying the right audience.

What to Do When You Realize You've Missed the Mark?

Ideally, you catch this as soon as possible. So, what do you do when your carefully planned campaign targets the wrong audience or, worse, causes harm to the intended one?

Time-out: Pause. Stop everything, re-evaluate, and then move forward again—depending on how severe the misstep is.

Refine the Message: If the audience isn't responding or is responding negatively, evaluate both the message and how it's being conveyed. If you've invested heavily in the campaign and can't change it, go back to step one. If changes can still be made, adjust the message to better fit the right audience as quickly as possible.

Additional Segmentation: Maybe you targeted too broad an audience? Try breaking your audience down into smaller subgroups (after analysis) and reach out to them with more specific messages that resonate.

Social Media: Own up to the mistake. Take responsibility. If that's too much for you, at least listen. Read both negative and positive feedback and use it to improve your messaging and audience targeting.

How to Spot a Misstep in Targeting as Early as Possible:

It's the Data, Stupid: Don't rely solely on social platforms. They may spread your ads where there's more activity, but that might not be your desired audience. Keep a close eye on your digital campaigns. Are the people you wanted to reach responding? If so, how are they responding? If it's not what you expected—reassess. If it's not your intended audience—reassess. If metrics are low across the board—reassess.

Social Monitoring: Tools like Brandwatch or Hootsuite help track real-time conversations about your brand. Look for discussions about your brand or campaign specifically.

A/B Testing: If you didn't start with this, reconsider your approach. It's the easiest way to understand if you've hit the mark with your audience—or not.

Surveys and Feedback Forms: Old-school, but effective. These take more time but are more in-depth. They can help you fine-tune your messages to avoid wasting money.

When it comes to audiences, it's best to research them thoroughly upfront. But if you've missed the mark, it happens. You're in good company. The most critical thing is how you react when it does.

4

EARLY STAGE? BUILD A STRONG(ER) VALUE PROPOSITION. IT'S WORTH IT

Did you know that 42% of startups fail because they didn't address a market need? A strong value proposition is essential for startup success, serving as the anchor for why customers choose you over the competition.

A value proposition is a clear statement explaining how your product solves customers' problems, delivers specific benefits, and tells your ideal customer why they should buy from you instead of someone else. It includes key elements: your target market, the specific benefits your product offers, and how your product is different from or better than the competition.

Unfortunately, many startups struggle with this. Often, it's due to a lack of customer insight, being too broad or vague, or ignoring the competition. Among the millions of tasks founders face, building a strong value proposition often takes a back seat.

To help you overcome that, here are some actionable steps for creating a strong value proposition:

1. Describe your idea clearly.

This may seem obvious, but it's not. Think of it as your elevator pitch—if you can't explain what you do clearly in one sentence, your potential customer won't understand either. Write a one-sentence summary of what your product does and who it helps. For example: "An app that helps remote teams stay connected through virtual coffee breaks." This shows your audience the problem your product solves and how it does it, in simple language anyone can understand.

2. Define your audience.

Identifying who will benefit from your product is crucial. Drill down to specifics: demographics, job titles, industries, etc. For example, remote workers and team managers in tech companies, ages 25-45, worldwide. If you think your solution can fit "everyone" or "any business with more than 10 employees," you're doing it wrong. A metal laser-cutting company with 15 employees has different needs from a biotech company with 15 employees. Define your audience carefully.

3. Talk to potential users.

Engage with potential users and get feedback. Join online

communities, forums, or social media groups related to your product. Observe discussions, ask questions, and gather insights on customer pain points and what they seek in a solution. Initially, ask for advice rather than pitching, to ensure they are open and honest with you.

4. Highlight your unique benefit.

Look at your competitors and identify what makes your idea stand out. Early on, focus on one main benefit that differentiates your product from others. For instance, while other apps may focus on productivity, your app may uniquely focus on social interaction to boost team morale.

5. Create and test your value proposition statement.

Use a basic template like: "We help [target audience] with [problem] by providing [solution]." Keep it short, aiming for one or two sentences. Test your statement with a small group of people and adjust based on their feedback. The simpler and more direct, the better.

Once you have a value proposition, set up regular feedback loops to refine it. A strong value proposition not only attracts customers but helps keep them.

5

BACK TO BASICS: ADVERTISING, MARKETING, AND AUDIENCE

Suddenly, the CEO or another senior executive says, "We need to advertise!" Here are the essential questions you need to ask:

1. Why?

Why "must we advertise?" What happened? Pinpoint the reason for the advertising push. When you refine the reason, finding effective and efficient solutions becomes much easier. Advertising is just one option in a marketing plan. Not everyone needs to advertise, and there are other strategies to consider. So, has something changed in the plan, environment, or market, or is it simply time for advertising as part of the strategy?

2. Who is the audience?

Audience analysis is one of the most crucial steps, and it's worth investing time and effort into. The more focused your audience, the easier everything else will become. Proper audience analysis will help you understand these two key things:

- **What bothers your audience? What's missing? What can you solve for them?**
- **Where is your audience, and how can you reach them?**

3. What do you want to say?

Or, more accurately, what do you want your audience to do? Once you know where your audience is and what bothers them, you'll know how to communicate your message so that the audience takes the desired action. Clarify exactly what you want your audience to do. This depends on your "marketing/sales" strategy. Are you looking for leads or demand? It's crucial to know which stage of the funnel your advertising targets. Be focused on the goals of the advertising.

4. How will you measure success?

If you don't measure, you won't know. Or you can just donate the money to me—the result will be the same. Decide in advance what you're going to measure and then determine whether you've achieved it.

These questions will lay the best foundation for any marketing activity, whether it's advertising, email campaigns, events, or more. The more accurate your answers to these questions, the more successful the campaign will be.

Practical Steps for Implementing These Questions

1. **Define your objectives:** Start by defining clear, measurable objectives. Are you aiming to increase brand awareness, generate leads, drive sales, or something else? Clear objectives will guide all your subsequent decisions.
2. **Conduct a deep audience research:** Use surveys, focus groups, and social media insights to understand your audience's needs, preferences, and behaviors. Develop detailed buyer personas that represent different segments of your target audience.
3. **Craft a compelling message:** Based on your audience research, develop a message that resonates with your audience's needs and desires. Ensure that the message is clear, concise, and aligns with your brand's voice and values.
4. **Select the right channels:** Choose the most effective channels to reach your audience. This could include social media platforms, email marketing, search engine advertising, and more. Consider where your audience spends their time and tailor your strategy accordingly.
5. **Plan your budget:** Allocate your budget based on the channels and tactics that will deliver the best ROI. Be prepared to adjust your budget as you monitor the performance of your campaigns.

6. **Create a timeline:** Develop a timeline for your campaign that outlines key milestones, deadlines, and responsibilities. This will help keep your team on track and ensure that your campaign is executed smoothly.
7. **Monitor and measure:** Use analytics tools to track the performance of your campaign in real time. Measure key metrics such as engagement, conversion rates, and ROI. Regularly review your data and make adjustments as needed to optimize your campaign.
8. **Analyze and report:** After your campaign concludes, conduct a thorough analysis to determine what worked and what didn't. Use this information to improve future campaigns and share your findings with your team and stakeholders.

Implementing these steps will help you create a structured and effective advertising campaign that aligns with your overall marketing strategy. By focusing on the fundamentals of why, who, what, and how, you can ensure that your efforts are targeted, measurable, and impactful.

SECTION 2: BUILDING AND ENGAGING YOUR AUDIENCE

6

THE IMPORTANCE OF MEASUREMENT: BACK TO BASICS—WHY MEASURE?

Why am I writing about measurement? In my conversations with friends, colleagues, and clients, I often encounter inadequate or even missing measurement practices. Sometimes, people fail to grasp the true importance of accurate measurement.

Why Measure?

Accurate measurement allows you to understand where successes occurred, identify problems, pinpoint areas for improvement, and perhaps even decide whether to change your entire strategy. When measurement is absent or incorrect, several issues arise—each equally significant (yes, I've measured that!):

Resource Waste.

Missed Profit Potential.

Audience Misunderstanding.

According to a HubSpot study, companies that don't measure their marketing activities waste 30-40% of their marketing budget on ineffective strategies.

Lack of measurement also leads to a lack of direction. You won't know what influences your audience, and worse, you might not even know who your audience is. Properly measuring activities inevitably leads to significant improvements and growth. It's all about focusing on proven strategies rather than guessing.

Measuring Gives Clarity

With accurate data, you can better understand your audience and tailor your content and messages to their language. A McKinsey study found that companies leveraging customer data outperform competitors by 85% in sales growth and over 25% in profits. Understanding your audience means knowing what to say, to whom, how, when, and where. That's the fundamental data for success.

Measurement isn't just a nice add-on; it's essential. But it's not just about measuring—it's about measuring the correct data. It might sound technical, but understanding which data you need to see is genuinely creative. There's the type of data that allows breakthroughs—reaching new audiences, creating new products, and advancing your business.

You might be familiar with this story:

During World War II, the British sought ways to protect their bombers because they were coming back with low survival rates. They sent soldiers to inspect the planes after each bombing run, marking on a photo where the planes sustained the most damage. These marked areas were crucial for reinforcing protection.

However, a mathematician named Abraham Wald stopped them and suggested looking at the areas on the plane that returned with the least damage. Those areas were the most critical (i.e., a bit more damage in those spots would cause the plane to crash or explode). The planes that didn't return had been hit in the engine, front, and tail sections, while the planes that returned were not hit in those sections. And those sections were finally reinforced. In this case, the data that was not measured was more important.

Don't Ignore the Data You Don't See

In summary, if a tree falls in the forest and you don't measure its noise, did it make a sound? Measurement isn't just a nice-to-have; it's the essential foundation. Better to measure than to wonder. Accurate measurement helps you course-correct, optimize your efforts, and identify what truly matters to your success.

7

5 TIPS ON GETTING YOUR MESSAGE OUT THERE!

On social media (LinkedIn included), it's hard to get readers to stop what they're doing (scrolling aimlessly) and concentrate on reading YOUR message. So, you try to get their attention first. Yes, there are many ways to do that, but none hold out for long as people get used to everything quite quickly.

#1 Get to the Point as Quickly as Possible**

If you can, write it down in the first sentence, as I did. If it's catchy enough – people will keep on reading. Remember that if you want new clients or followers, they don't know you yet, so starting off a long story with the message at the end won't work on them. It will work on people who already know you, and those are mostly the only ones who comment and reply.

#2 Write Each Post as if the Readers See Your Page/Name for the First Time**

Remember that people got lazy since the internet and smartphones appeared, so they won't be bothered by actually DOING something for a brand or person they do not know. So, make it easy for them.

#3 Each Public Post Needs to Be a Stand-Alone Piece of Information**

This means: put your contact details at the end of each post. Don't let people search – or they'll just move on. As I've said earlier, people have become lazy, so even if they see a great tip, or joke, or product, they'll mumble something to themselves and carry on.

#4 Tell Them What to Do**

It's not as if people are stupid, but research has shown that when scrolling aimlessly on social media, people tend to have zombie-like attitudes. So, when giving them a clear call to action – they act. Seriously. And it happens to everyone (it's the research, not me), no matter what race, IQ, status, gender, etc. Tell people what to do – like, comment, click, etc.

#5 Decide Where the Main Message Is – in the Text or in the Visual/Video**

If your text holds the main message – find a visual that does not take the center of attention. If your visual/video holds the main message – keep the text short and simple. Have one message only per post.

8

THE MEANING OF A HOOK IN A PITCH AND HOW TO CHOOSE THE RIGHT ONE

Let's talk about hooks and why they're essential for any pitch. Whether you're pitching a startup, asking for a raise, selling a product, or even presenting a vacation plan to friends, the hook is what grabs attention and keeps people listening.

The Power of the First Sentence

Much like when you meet someone, those first few words often determine whether they want to continue the conversation. The same goes for your audience during any pitch.

So, think about it—what is your audience thinking after hearing your first sentence? Without a compelling hook, the rest of your pitch might not matter. Data shows that if you don't engage them right away, you risk losing their attention entirely.

Why Is the Hook So Important?

Your goal is to keep the audience engaged, and this can be challenging, especially if:

- You're not the first speaker.
- Your audience isn't familiar with your field.

To overcome this, you need a hook that is both appropriate for your audience and strong enough to prompt action.

6 Types of Hooks and When to Use Them:

- The Surprising Statistic Hook

A shocking or interesting statistic grabs attention—if it's relevant. Example:

"Gartner found that 60% of businesses waste money on ineffective campaigns."

- The Question Hook

Ask a question that addresses your audience's pain point, making them eager for your solution. Example:

"What if you could double your sales in six months without increasing expenses?"

- The Personal Story Hook

Stories resonate emotionally. Research shows people remember information better when it's conveyed through a story. Example:

"Last year, I faced the same problem many of you are dealing with right now..."

- The Problem-Solution Hook

Nothing grabs attention faster than addressing a common problem and offering a solution. Example:

"Businesses spend over 20 hours a month on manual task entry. Our software automates that process in a quarter of the time."

- The Visionary Hook

Sell a dream that's grounded in reality. Example:

"Imagine if, instead of commuting every day, your office could come to you wherever you are."

- The Humoristic Hook

Humor can be an excellent icebreaker, but it must fit the audience and the context. Example:

"Remember when everything took twice as long? With our software, your coffee breaks will finally last longer than your to-do list."

- Can You Use More Than One Hook?

You might think, "Why not combine several hooks?" But you shouldn't. You have one shot to hook your audience, and there's a fine line between 'wow' and 'get to the point.' Dragging the hook out, even by one sentence, risks losing their attention.

The Key to a Good Hook

A great hook depends on two things:

- What you're trying to achieve.
- Who your audience is.

So, always visualize your audience—what will they think after hearing your first sentence?

9

A GOLDFISH, AN ELEVATOR, AND YOUR BUSINESS

If you can get your elevator pitch through to a goldfish, then you know you've got it.

Okay, the goldfish's short memory span is a myth, but it's a good one to practice with. In today's fast-paced world, you have between 7 to 10 seconds to grab attention with your elevator pitch, which is not much —with or without the myth —so use them wisely.

Having an effective elevator pitch isn't just a necessity for startups; it's crucial for established companies as well. Whether you're launching a new product, introducing a new service, or simply refining your messaging, a concise and compelling elevator pitch can make all the difference.

And today, you'll be needing that elevator pitch not only for investors, sales, or marketing but also to recruit new employees at any level.

A strong pitch is a one-stop-shop for what you are and

what you can do. A good one grabs attention, conveys your value, and makes the listener want to know more. That's the point —getting them to want to know more. That's the true meaning of a good elevator pitch—not sales.

Here are several tips to help you craft a strong elevator pitch:

1. Define Your Audience.

To make a good elevator pitch, you will need several versions, and defining your audience is the most important first step. Doing this correctly will make the rest of the process much easier. When defining an audience, consider factors such as size, income, job, lifestyle, location, and more. For B2B, drill down to position, decision-making authority, pain points, goals, competitors, and more. Create a unique persona per audience, and tailor a specific pitch to suit each one.

2. Keep It Short and Simple.

One common mistake is making the pitch too long or overly complex. If it lasts more than 60 seconds or is packed with details, you risk losing your audience's attention. For example:

"Our company, founded in 2010, has developed a highly intricate platform that integrates various APIs to streamline business processes, optimize workflows, and increase overall efficiency by an average of 35%, according to a recent internal survey conducted over three quarters."

While informative, this is overwhelming. Instead, aim for clarity and brevity:

"We provide a cloud-based platform that helps small businesses automate their invoicing, saving them time and reducing errors."

This version communicates the core message without overwhelming the listener. Focus on what you do and how you help.

3. Stay Focused.

Avoid trying to cover too many points in your pitch. For instance, saying,

"We offer consulting, digital marketing services, software development, and HR solutions for businesses of all sizes in every industry," is ineffective. Instead, a more focused pitch will have greater impact:

"We help mid-sized tech companies scale efficiently by integrating tailored digital marketing strategies, innovative software solutions, and streamlined HR processes."

This example is clear and easy to understand.

4. Practice.

Even the best-crafted pitch can fall flat if it's not delivered well. Rehearse your pitch in front of a mirror, with a friend, or record yourself to watch and learn.

5. Start With a Strong Hook.

The first few seconds are critical. Instead of starting with a generic statement, consider opening with something that immediately engages your listener, such as:

"Did you know that 60% of small businesses struggle with late payments? Our platform solves that."

This kind of opening grabs attention and immediately sets the stage for the unique value your product or service offers. But make sure your hook aligns with your audience's pain points—if they don't struggle with payments, this approach will miss the mark.

Bonus Tip:

If possible, practice your pitch on an audience you wouldn't mind losing. If it doesn't work, talk with them afterward to understand what went wrong—it could be a wrong pain point, lack of confidence, or being too long. Use the feedback to perfect your pitch for the audiences that matter most.

Conclusion:

A well-crafted elevator pitch is crucial for both startups and established companies. Whether pitching a new product, service, or your entire company, keeping your pitch concise, highlighting your unique value, and tailoring it to your audience can make all the difference. As Guy Kawasaki says, "Keep it simple, stupid." Focus on clarity, brevity, and value, and you'll see results.

10

MARKETING: BE THE MARKET STALL, NOT THE DISPLAY WINDOW

I'll start with what you should take away from this post: treat your social activity as if it were a market stall and not as if it's a display window.

A display window is where you present your products, services, advertisements, and whatnot. Your customers (or potential customers) look at the display window and decide if they want "to buy or not to buy." A big mistake businesses make is treating social networks as just another advertising asset where they can publish information to "the public" and get it over with. They are missing the essence of social networking, which is being... well, social.

A store window, just like advertising, is a one-way information pipe from shop owner to customer. Social networks, on the other hand, are bi-directional, where information moves from either side. Your responsibility, as a business, is to listen, adapt, talk, and converse.

The #1 mistake is not listening to what you hear from customers. It could be simple questions where answering them would grant you a world of gratitude from your potential customers, and also from your past/paying customers. It can also lower spending on customer service. We all know that having a good opinion of your company does not end at the cashier, so you need to keep an eye and ear on paying customers as much as potential ones. If all you want is a one-way audience, just use normal ads and don't waste money on a social team. But that's a mistake.

The Market Stall

Think of yourself walking down a market with all the smells, colors, and produce just popping up around you. It looks just like a shop display window, doesn't it? Well, that's where the stall owners come in.

They interact with you. You interact with them. You ask questions, they give you information. Some give you samples. The good ones even give you more than what you came for. They give you added value, for example, tips on how best to eat this fruit or vegetable, how to pick the tastiest one, etc. You start liking them and listening to them, and keep interacting – usually, you find yourself paying more than you planned to, and what's more important - next time you're looking for these fruits, you will probably go back to the same stall.

This interaction generates several outcomes:

- It provides higher confidence in what you're buying and whom you're buying from. You might return to the same market stall another day.
- It will also get "stuck" in the client's Top Of Mind (TOM) area, so the client might turn into your "unintentional" salesperson among their friends, family, and social media.

Of course, this could backfire if the salesperson behind the stall does a bad job, treats you badly, badmouths, lies, etc.

Your Stall

What will make you stand out from the crowd of other stalls? The magic marketing triangle is: Who is your audience? -> What is your message? -> Who are you?

Audience: If you do not know your audience, you might as well give your product or service away for free. You have to know your audience inside and out; create multiple personas, understand where to find them, what they like, what their pain points are, etc.

Your Message: "Come buy" is not a message. I mean, it could be, but it's a short-term message and it relates to a shop display window. Think 'conversation starters,' not 'messages.' Take your (or your company's) goals, align them with your audience's pain points, and cut your main conversation starter from there. Then, create small tactical starters to spread along the way.

You: Your company also needs a persona. Who is the person behind the market stall interacting with customers? Are they a shouter? Are they 'cool'? Are they formal or informal? Finding your own marketing persona on social media will help you build the tone and voice of your company. The basic rule is consistency. Have the same tone and voice spread across all your outlets.

So, How Can Your Stall Stand Out Among the Others?

1. **Make More Noise Than Others** Yes. Yelling out your products is what you need to do. The trick is to yell smartly. This means understanding who is walking past your stall (the audience) and researching how your marketing activity looks and sounds, the visual and audio elements, the amount of text, and the amount you spend.
2. **Share Valuable Content** The second trick is what you yell. Or, in better terms - what are you giving your customers? Every fruit stall will shout the price of their watermelon, but you will be the one giving out samples. You will be the one giving out recipes for watermelon shakes. The more

customers feel they receive valuable content, the more loyal they will be and spend more money.

3. **Innovation** There is no such thing as "I have no content." Every company has content. All you need to do is curate it and edit it. For example, the questions you get on your customer service side – that is content, both question and answer. Yes, even opening hours.

11

MARKETING FROM DAY ONE - WHY IT'S IMPORTANT TO INVOLVE MARKETERS FROM THE START

Marketing should be involved from day one. From the moment the idea is conceived for a service, product, or process.

Why? Because good marketers are, first and foremost, good thinkers. They should have a process in their mind that can serve as a sounding board for focusing, alignment, precision, and deep understanding of what you're selling, to whom, and what your messaging is.

A good idea isn't always enough. Translating the idea into a message aimed at the right audience at the right time can be the catalyst for success. And by "audience," I don't just mean buyers. I also mean seed investors or Series A investors... so your audience changes with the stage your business is in. Even if the product or service isn't ready yet, marketers can still play a crucial role.

For each 'audience,' a separate messaging process is built. This refines the product or service and prepares the ground for fundraising if necessary or for the product/service's market entry. Until then, marketers promote the brand, the company, and the founders, while exploring and educating the market. They identify what's missing and cushion the landing of the new product or service.

Why do startups fail?

The primary reason for startup failure is that there's no market need for the product/service. This is often due to insufficient initial research. Once the research is done and a market need is identified, other reasons for startup failures include, in descending order:,running out of money and/or lack of investor interest, an unsuitable startup team, stronger competitors, and various other factors.

It's surprising to find that over 35% of startups don't yet have a website, while more than 75% of customers and investors (across all markets and sectors) check out the product/service/brand through the website, making it an essential part of their research (based on research by Mayple).

According to most statistics websites, 'no need' and 'no money' interchangeably occupy the first and second spots, together accounting for over 70% of the reasons for failures.

Marketing professionals can help at every stage, and good

marketing professionals can make the difference needed to overcome these common reasons for failure.

1. **Market Research for Genuine Need:** Good marketers can help refine the idea and assist with market research. Knowing how to ask, who to ask, and how to interpret the answers and data. Good quality information often becomes clear when reading between the lines and fully understanding the audience.
2. **Out of Money or No Investor Interest:** What is marketing? It's researching and understanding the audience you need at this stage, and knowing how to refine messages that resonate with them to prompt the desired action. Pretty simple, right? Even here, good marketers will identify the right audience and craft the right messages. The foundation is creating a tailored sales presentation or set of targeted messages for each investor, client, and audience. There's no one-size-fits-all presentation. A venture capital fund brings its values, while corporate venture capital (CVC) has different values. A private investor will seek entirely different values, and so forth. Each pitch must be personalized for the audience it is presented to. It's a lot of work, but worth the effort.
3. **An Unsuitable Startup Team:** Understanding the audience and crafting messages also extends

internally into the company. Building job postings and managing recruitment processes from the messaging and emphasis perspective can make a difference in recruiting the right people.

4. **Digital Presence and Brand Presence:** A digital presence and brand presence in the right circles are critical for any company, even more so for a startup. Yes, it's part of the budget, but if a tree falls in the forest and no one hears it – did it really fall?

What I want you to take away from this is that what many see as "we'll handle it later" can lead to a situation where there's no "later."

SECTION 3: ENHANCING CUSTOMER EXPERIENCE

12

CUSTOMER EXPERIENCE, HOTELS, AND MARKETING TAKEAWAYS

A bit about one of the more tangible aspects of marketing - customer experience. Each of us is a customer of some brand, and we know more or less when the customer experience is positive and when it is negative. Whether our feeling is justified or not is another question.

What I want to convey here is that as marketers, our "worries" are bigger than the customer experience that the brand/product/service (hereinafter "the brand" :-)) provides directly. From a marketing perspective, customer experience is a whole set of touchpoints with the product, be it directly or indirectly. Therefore, when a brand wants to provide us with a customer experience, it needs to think outside the box and look at the customer experience and everything that goes with it from a distance.

The Hotel Example

Here is an example I experienced in a hotel. A five-star hotel with excellent service, a smiling and supportive staff, delicious meals, top-notch facilities, clean and tidy rooms, in short - the highest possible customer experience. It is indeed worth five stars. So what's the problem? Customer experience is not just the hotel. Customer experience is a holistic view of... well... the customer experience.

So, when the windows in the room are thin and not sealed, every car that passes on the road will wake up the guest (not me, of course; I sleep like a log).

One can argue that a car on the road, a garbage truck in the morning, or just teenagers who don't fall asleep until 3 am are not the fault or responsibility of the hotel. And they are right, but the hotel needs... no, must, take into account all the factors that can affect the customer experience, whether they are its responsibility or not. If they are its responsibility, it can easily fix, compromise, and change. If they are not its responsibility, there are a variety of solutions that can alleviate the "problem" and improve the customer experience. Starting with double windows, a reduced price for rooms on the side of the road, and more.

Again, you are right that the hotel does not need to worry about everything, but at the end of the day the review of the hotel will be - "Excellent, but next to a noisy road." And that is why it is important for marketers to "go out into the field."

Going Out into the Field

Whether it is to the stores where our products are sold, to the customer service department in the company, to be attached to the sales department (and even be a salesperson), to be on the websites where our campaigns appear, and more.

Going out into the field is half the action, and the other half is data. Marketing needs to track the information that comes from customers and the media, to see where our brand appears, what affects it, what overshadows or strengthens it, and more, in order to understand if there is a problem that is not its responsibility but affects the brand, and also if there is room to improve the customer experience in these places.

Data-Driven Customer Experience

Customer experience doesn't end with direct interaction with the brand. It extends to every touchpoint, from the noise outside a hotel room to the usability of a product. For marketers, this means being vigilant about the entire customer journey. The hotel example underscores the importance of considering factors beyond immediate control.

Steps to Enhance Customer Experience:

1. **Identify External Factors:** Determine what external factors could negatively impact the customer experience. This could be environmental

noise, third-party services, or even indirect interactions like delivery services.

2. **Develop Mitigation Strategies:** Once identified, develop strategies to mitigate these factors. This could involve physical changes (like better windows), alternative solutions (like offering quieter room options), or even clear communication about potential issues (like informing guests about nearby construction).
3. **Engage with Customers:** Collect feedback directly from customers to understand their experiences and identify areas for improvement. Use surveys, reviews, and direct interactions to gather insights.
4. **Analyze Data:** Use data analytics to track customer feedback, identify trends, and measure the impact of external factors on customer satisfaction. This can help prioritize which issues to address first.
5. **Implement Continuous Improvement:** Make customer experience a continuous improvement process. Regularly review feedback and data, and make incremental changes to enhance the overall experience.

Conclusion:

Customer experience is a critical component of marketing that goes beyond direct interactions. It encompasses every touchpoint, direct and indirect, that a customer has with a brand. By going out into the field and collecting data, marketers can identify and mitigate external factors that impact customer experience, ensuring that the brand delivers a consistently positive experience.

13

CUSTOMER LOYALTY IS NOT A PRIVILEGE. IT'S A NECESSITY

Old-School Marketing vs. Today's Sophisticated Customer

In the old marketing approach ("message marketing"), loyalty meant customers who made repeat purchases. "If they bought from me again, they're loyal. So, let's make them come back by offering promotions, discounts, and gifts." Today's customers are much more sophisticated than that.

Customer Loyalty Is Built on Process and Strategy

Customer loyalty is built primarily through the process, stemming from the company's marketing strategy. This process comprises touchpoints between the company and the customer, which largely determine whether the customer will be loyal or not. If there aren't enough touchpoints in the current process, the company must create them. And not just any touchpoints but ones that provide value to the customer.

Incentives Alone Aren't Enough

According to Protiviti, marketers and business owners are starting to realize that "reward technologies" like Groupon, points, bonuses, etc., aren't the way to enhance loyalty. They're just part of the process. Protiviti found that 2012 and 2013 would be years of understanding the need for genuine loyalty and building it without relying solely on rewards and gifts.

A survey by Loyalty 360 found that 78% of customers would feel more loyal if their purchasing experience was positive. And it starts with the first touchpoint—advertising. It continues through subsequent touchpoints, from who answers the phone (or stands at the point of sale) to handing over the receipt/invoice and the customer's relationship with the product at home (usage, customer service, etc.). The purchasing process is crucial in building loyalty.

Look at the Newspaper Distributors Tomorrow Morning

How are they dressed? How do they behave? What do they say when they hand you the paper? These seemingly "unimportant" points in the company's eyes are among the most important in the customer's eyes.

So What Strengthens or Creates Customer Loyalty?

As always, it starts with the audience (consumers, customers, and other descriptors). The company must learn about its customers. You need to find out why they choose to buy from you or not. What are their needs?

Leverage Social Media for Customer Insights

Today, it's much easier to understand your customer through social media (which must be embedded in your marketing strategy, but that's another story). Through the right conversations, you can learn a lot about your company's image and your existing and potential audiences.

Rewards and Promotions: Means, Not Ends

I'm not dismissing the use of rewards and promotions, but I emphasize that they should be means, not ends. You can learn much more about the customer through promotions.

Non-Traditional Rewards

Rewards don't always have to be products. Some companies will find that customers enjoy unique product experiences much more, such as:

- Off-road driving courses for off-road vehicle buyers

- Front-row seats at a fashion show for fashion customers
- A cookbook from of a famous chef teaching proper kitchen equipment use for kitchen/baking product buyers
- Photography courses for camera buyers
- And many more ideas

These types of rewards increase loyalty to the company or brand.

Personalized Offers and Engagement

Customers are no longer just numbers in a system; they're people with names, families, important dates, hobbies, and more. Analyze your existing customers from time to time and approach them personally (as much as possible) to offer tailored promotions. No more "5% off a repeat purchase," but "Buy the complementary product for what you bought yesterday."

In the Digital Space

Provide information that doesn't require a purchase. Share tips, photos, and news from around the world. All these contribute to increased loyalty. Build a strong presence.

Top-Down Implementation Is Essential

Implementing this new marketing method must start from the top and trickle down to the security guard at the entrance to the building or store. Every member of the organization should be aligned with this customer-centric approach.

14

AUTOMATION IS IMPORTANT, BUT DON'T FORGET THE HUMAN TOUCH

From Chaplin to Chatbots

Since the 1930s, when Charlie Chaplin worked on the assembly line in the film *Modern Times*, it's been clear that the world is heading toward automation in every field. But unlike most fears, new technology does not wipe out jobs; it replaces them with new types of jobs. Yes, there is a transition in which people find themselves unemployed due to automation, but over the course of a decade, it's a small price to pay as new jobs emerge.

In B2C markets, automation is designed to accompany the customer throughout the purchase journey. The buzz is so big that sometimes it feels as if automation has become the goal rather than the means. There's a rush toward marketing and sales automation, with technology and bots being used to lure customers in. Could this craze ultimately hurt us?

Research Insights: Automation and the Human Touch

A study from Harvard Business School in the early 2020s uncovered some interesting insights into customers and automation. The main takeaway is that a human touch in the purchasing process, even if only an option, leads to more conversions.

Let's start with a few pointers:

- The research was conducted in the financial/insurance/loan sector, not the consumer market.
- The study focused on measuring anxiety levels among users with and without human interaction rather than directly assessing the impact of human touch on purchasing. So, the conclusions were drawn from research that didn't initially aim to measure the effects of human interaction on purchasing behavior.
- The study's audience was relatively mature, so further analysis is needed for younger age groups.

Research and Data

Participants were asked to update their investment portfolio at a specific financial institution, but only some were given access to assistance during the process (they weren't given help directly, just the option to request it).

The results showed that people felt uneasy about their

decisions without human interaction, even if their financial outcomes were better than expected. The participants most satisfied with their decisions were those who had access to human assistance—even if they didn't use it. This suggests that simply providing access to human support reduces customer anxiety.

A closer look revealed that only 15% of participants actually used the option for human help.

Two Groups, Two Different Text Messages

Both groups received a text message after completing a specific step in the funding application process:

- **Group 1:** "Thanks for signing up. If you have any questions, contact me at 050-0000000."
- **Group 2:** "Thanks for signing up."

The group that was given the option to reach out to a real person was 80% likely to continue with the funding application process. The second group was only 64% likely to continue.

The Takeaway

Even with companies' need for automation, we can't ignore the importance of personal and human connections in improving conversion rates. This emphasis on the human touch is evident mostly in bank or insurance ads. As the study suggests, banks realized that human interaction reduces anxiety, minimizes uncertainty, and helps close more deals, at least in the financial sector. How this applies to other fields remains to be seen.

In Conclusion

As my dad says: "There's nothing like your personal banker, even if now I live an hour and a half away." Yes, he moved to another part of the country but hasn't left his bank (not just the brand but his personal banker).

The study was conducted by Michelle A. Shell and Verian V. Buel of Harvard Business School.

15

CONTENT, A TREE, AND MAKING MONEY

If a tree falls in the forest and no one hears it, does it still make a sound?

Please don't. "A falling tree through the air creates airwaves that..." me. I'm being metaphorical here.

So, if you create a great piece of content, but no one is around to consume it, is it any good? Creating good content does not end when your masterpiece is finished. That's only the beginning. If you don't care about someone consuming your content, then you're an artist, doing it for your soul and not for money. That's a whole other article.

Content-Audience-Distribution-Monetization

These four elements are the basic pillars of making money from content. To some of you, this may come as a surprise, but you will need to make money from content; otherwise, there won't be anyone around to hear the tree fall.

Content

First, you need to determine what type of content creator you need. There are basically two types: the writer and the content person, or the artists and the empathizers.

- **The Writer:** The writer usually writes to let their emotions and energy out. Many write beautifully and captivatingly, but their work often ends up "in the drawer," never to be seen again. Some go on to be painters, singers, songwriters, authors, and other artists. These individuals create for themselves, and their followers find them. They do not change their "art" to accommodate others. They can also be hated for their work, and it will still be okay for them.
- **The Content Person:** Content persons usually create for others and need feedback. They create something that "talks" to others, like comedians on stage, actors on the screen, and so on. So, if your best friend tells you about his roommate who writes great stories, and even you enjoy reading them, it does not mean he can create content that sells. To make money from content, you need content persons.

Audience

Good content persons create for others, so they MUST know their audience. They need to tell a story that will end in an action taken by the audience. The content created does not need to be long-form. A social media post or an image in the right place is sufficient.

Audience research is a must. Research by checking out the competition, joining groups, digital channels, blogs, etc. Getting the right audience and understanding it is more than 50% of the work. If you work hard on your tree but bring a busload of deaf people to the forest, they won't hear your tree fall. They are not your audience.

Distribution

Marketing (which is almost a synonym for content professionals) is responsible for getting the right people you found in your audience research to the forest so they can listen to the tree falling. "Be where your audience is." That's Marketing Basics 101. How to get the message out there.

This "how" includes many other questions. The "how" to reach my audience question also includes what to use to get my message across. Should I use text? Video? And more questions that fall under the category of the technical side of content. In time, you should have a system of what works best, or you may have already been handed your company's holy book of "what works and what doesn't." Use it, but never be afraid of trying out new stuff, old stuff, things that never worked before, and weird stuff. People change, and so does how they consume content.

Monetization

Now that you have your correct audience in the forest and around your tree, you need to stop and think to yourself, 'if I do this for free, I might feel good about myself now, but I won't have any money to do it again.' So, now it's time to figure out how to make money out of this audience.

Monetization is a giant world of millions of service providers, ad exchanges, CPM, RPM, CPCs, and many other abbreviations. You need the money so you can continue to create another day.

Each pillar you read here has its own world with experts who are best at what they do. You need to gather them up to build the best team that will increase your income. These are the four pillars of making money from content. Use them well and take time to research them all with the same effort. Do not neglect any of these pillars; to make it work, they all need to have the same significance.

16

SOCIAL MEDIA, CUSTOMER SUPPORT, AND MONEY

Doing Your Social Media Right – Will Save You Money and Headaches

Small and medium-sized businesses (SMBs) and larger companies around the globe have yet to fully grasp the full potential of social media. Social media has almost reached maturity, and it took more than seven years for marketing people to understand what can be done with it. I'm not talking about advertising on social media. That's easy. I'm talking about using social media to your company's advantage for long-term brand building, nurturing good reviews, and making customers want to be near you so they can spend money on you.

As you know, there are two (legitimate) ways of making more money – increasing income and cutting expenses. Increasing income is a whole different ball game, and I won't play it now. I would like to emphasize the "cutting expenses" part of social media, and while doing so, strengthening your company's good image, gaining your customers' respect, making you a thought leader in your field, and in the long term – increasing your income like a snowball, but in a good sense.

The Biggest Mistake

The biggest mistake I have seen executives make about social media is underestimating it. And I mean really underestimating it. If they can't see, at the end of the day, an income line in their Excel sheet made by social media, then they believe it doesn't do anything, so they lower investments and manpower in that department.

True, many marketing executives do understand, and you might be one of them, but still, most industries are dominated by old-school people. They may be doing well, but with social media, they could be doing so much more. Social media is a long-term investment. Again, I'm not talking about advertising on social media, which could increase income right here and now.

The Problem

Most companies treat social media simply as another media outlet. Another media to show off their advertising and how good they are. Many believe that social media has lost its social touch, so they keep on using it as another TV screen.

This mistake is usually made by those old-school executives I talked about before. They give social media a try but can't see the impact it has in the short term, so they stop trying.

Your social media must create an ecosystem or a community run by you, creating conversations with your followers and customers. Of course, it depends on what type of brand you have, but usually, people need interaction with the brand they love or want to love. Having a social media page that has no conversation and only pumps out advertising and self-praise is wasting time and money on social media.

In addition to that, companies do not understand the power of social media. Social media is the first encounter between a brand and its customers or potential customers, and it happens more and more on mobile. If your social media is run by your niece's 20-year-old son, that is the impression your customers will have of you. Think of social media as your storefront or showcase. If your showcase storefront is designed badly, sales stay low. Social media is what your customers go to first – treat it as such.

Down to Business – VAC (Value Added Content)

If social media is run correctly, companies could cut expenses in other customer-facing departments. If social media is run correctly, companies could cut expenses in advertising and PR. If your company doesn't do that yet, here's a test you could do in your company that could get you a fat bonus:

Go down to customer support and get a list of the 10 FAQs, then make a list of the 10 most common complaints, and if there are any compliments, get them as well. From these lists, build short and easy-to-read social media posts and blogs or even social media landing pages. Start pumping these FAQs on social media. Try it for four weeks and then visit customer support again and evaluate the numbers. Was there a lower number of calls? Did the callers notice the social media FAQs? Did any of them use them? Etc.

If you have more "say" in your company, record a call waiting recording that tells callers about the social media FAQs. Guide your customer support people to tell callers about the social media FAQs.

FAQs are VAC. User manuals are VAC. Maintenance tips are VAC. "Our experts tell their secrets" is VAC. Etc. The more VAC your customers and potential customers get, the more you become a thought leader – the more good reviews you get – the more trust you gain – the more money you make. It's that simple. Long-term, but simple.

Your only "hard" decisions are how to get all that VAC to the people out there. Videos? Articles? Photos? White papers? Etc.

Here are 5 social mistakes I still see happening!

Like Canada's Justin Trudeau said: "It's 2015." It is, but there are still a number of places where 2008 marketing behaviors rule.

I can still find many SMBs holding on to outdated social behaviors. Here are the five biggest mistakes that can still be found on social platforms:

1. **I Know Best.** The "I" can refer to the brand owner/head of marketing or to the person operating the social media, who wrongly believes that their way is the only way. The social platform is a community center. And as in a community, you share. Your community members converge around you to get added value and also to feel part of your brand world. You cannot talk down to your community and treat them as if they are students and you are the headmaster. A smart brand will be a part of the discussion and not just a message board. Sometimes, great ideas come from your community. Listen.
2. **Me, Me, Me.** You have a sale. You have news. You have a great design. You have a great whatever. Yes, we know. You also have narcissism. A strong brand can talk about anything, share anything, and show anything. A strong brand does not need to talk about itself all the time. Of course, don't forget to say how great you are and do show off, but don't make showing off your only social activity. People get tired of it very quickly.
3. **I Can't Say.** A strong brand has nothing to hide. Many SMBs are afraid to publicly share prices.

Don't be. If you are sure of the value you have to offer and you have been working on showing that value to potential customers, then you have nothing to fear by posting your price. If you don't feel sure about posting your price, then you have a problem. And people will feel that. Be sure of your pricing and value – don't hide the price.

4. **You're All the Same to Me.** No. People are not the same. The only thing that can be said about your entire social community as an entity is that they like your brand, and that's why they are here. Never treat your community as one homogenous entity. If you get interaction from 50% of your community, that means you are missing out on potentially another 50%. Try different approaches to reach different audiences who have in common one thing – you (your brand). It will also show that your brand is dynamic and changing, which is what makes a brand interesting. And when a brand is interesting, it gets more interaction. More interaction leads to more revenue.
5. **Referrals.** This is not a BIG mistake, and it is still being researched, but I believe that SMBs should give all information on their social page and not send people off to a website. People come to the social platform to interact – ask and get answered. Being sent to a website (or other off-social platform location) could discourage people from

continuing to interact with you. Think about yourself asking a waiter in a restaurant what is recommended, and all the waiter does is tell you to look at the menu. That's bad social interaction. The menu will sell a dish; a good waiter can sell a full meal. As much as you can, keep talking to your community in the social realm.

17

5 TIPS ON MAKING YOUR CUSTOMER HAPPY USING EASY CONTENT TRICKS

This is so amazing because it's not only making their journey better, it also shortens it, enhances your company's image, turns your customers into the best salespersons, and, better yet, reduces expenses! So much for so little! Wow, shut up and take my money

Unfortunately, for many years, content has always been put aside as a nice-to-have part of the marketing team. In practical terms, it means that content positions were usually low-pay roles with a "just write what I tell you" attitude. Only recently has content started to gain more power as a game changer, as consumers are getting more and more fed up with the usual sales and marketing tactics thrown at them day by day and are looking for some storytelling to light up their imagination. Yes, even when buying toilet paper.

If you're raising your eyebrows and telling me that content has always been important in your company, hold it. I don't mean advertising or amazing Super Bowl spots, or "buy one, get one free" promotions. I mean content! Real value-adding content. Stuff that people actually take into consideration and remember, and sometimes even use that content themselves.

It's the Added Value, Dummy!

There is a huge difference between "Thanks for buying our product" and "Thanks for buying our product, and here's what you can do with it." Added value is the difference. When we pay money for a product but get more (or the feeling of more), we are happy. When we get the product and start using it with no added hassle, we are happy. When we find out that we can do more than we planned with the product, we are happy.

There are many times when consumers should be happy but are not. It might be due to not understanding the product or service, difficulty getting help, or simply being uninformed about the product or service.

Usually, it comes down to missing information, which often happens after you have paid for the product or service.

Information is king and costs money, true. But there is soooo much information out there that you need to control the flow of it, thus making it cheap and cost-effective. How?

By spreading it like powdered sugar along the customer's journey.

How many calls or online questions do you get about your product that are very simple to answer? How many potential customers have you missed out on while answering these "stupid questions"?

Make Your Content Work for You

Let's take TicTac. Did you know that the box itself has a built-in way of getting just one TicTac out every time? (It's not the issue here, so if you didn't know that, look it up on Google.) But the thing is that there is so much information out there that could add value to your product.

Another example is Leatherman multi-tools. Their best-selling tool is called Wave. Many do not know that it has a hidden lanyard ring so you could secure your Wave with a piece of rope or a keychain (It's not really a hidden feature, but it's tucked inside so deep that you really have to know about it to use it). Yes, it could be written on the box in small print, but who reads that? The small print is so legal and formal and such a party-pooper. Oh, you've added some really important information in the same text size? No thank you.

Every company has tons of lost information just lying on the floor and waiting to be picked up and used. And so much of it is so easy and cheap to distribute to your customers or potential customers. So, let's go:

5 Tips

1- Start with the Basics

Wherever you can, make your contact information easy to find and readable. When online, make it linkable/usable (links to maps or phone calls, etc.). When you give out your contact info, it makes people secure. They feel that, when the time comes, they will have someone to talk to, even when most won't ever contact you. So share as many means of contacting you as possible, and make sure it is easily found—on your social media pages, website, emails, receipts, user manuals, packaging, on the product itself if possible, and any other contact point your company has with humans.

2- Visit Your Customer Service Department

Collect all the reasons people contacted your company. Some may be complaints or positive suggestions. Use data and statistics to see what sticks out. Often, it's a simple question of opening hours or "how tos" about your product or service that consumes much-needed time from your customer service team. Think about the common "disconnect the cable, count to 10, connect the cable" type of calls. If this was written somewhere visible and easy to find on the product or on the website as a "Do this before you call us" sticker, think how many service calls and wasted time would have been saved! Find a way to communicate what you find in your customer service department to all customers—especially to those who have not yet asked and to new/potential customers. Use websites, social media, emails, user-friendly manuals, packaging info, easy-to-read Ikea-style printables, or whatever works. Take another step forward and create a 'How To' page on your site and communicate it to your customers. You'll find that your customer service employees start dealing with "regular" customer service issues, have more time for each customer, and maybe you could make that department smaller. All in all, it will improve your company's image and customer services.

3- Sharable Q&A Page

If you don't have a Q&A page, create one for your company. Now comb the web for mentions about your product/company/competitors and see why you were mentioned. Answer these mentions and reference your Q&A page when you can. This serves several goals: you show that you care, they get an answer, and you send them to your website. Create the Q&A page to be a bit more appealing, like a landing page. Give the design and content some thought.

4- Reduce Text, Increase Visuals

People do not read the small print, so make it easier for them. Make the most important "small print" into big icons with headlines only, for example: DOES NOT FIT THESE

COFFEE MACHINES: X, Y, Z. If you let your customer find out a 'small print' issue at home—AFTER he paid for the service or product—you have lost him forever and gained another angry customer on your customer service line. This course of action will also reduce the number of customer service calls (the ones that make you wonder, 'why didn't they look it up on Google?!'). For example, a digital wristwatch. Have the watch features easily displayed on the box/printable and at the store itself as a small A5 pamphlet: How deep can I dive with it? Can I mute it? How to update the DST? And many other questions people have AFTER they throw away the fat and tiny user manual no one ever reads anyway. Find out the most common questions and display them on a small printed Ikea-style manual.

5- Hands-On

Every now and then, talk to one or two customers who have received help from your company. Find out what made the customer call, why, and what they did. What could have helped them? What could have prevented them from calling? Did they share their frustration online? If so, why? Were they approached by a customer service rep. or did they wait? How long did they wait, etc.? Also, try to find out how each step made them feel. That's key. Now find a happy customer and do the same with them. Identify your company's weak points and address them.

5.5 Bonus: Take the Journey Yourself

Be a customer, but choose a different persona—be the most annoying customer you have ever met. With this persona, start the journey. You might find that you can ease or shorten another process.

SECTION 4: CREATIVITY AND INNOVATION IN MARKETING

18

STORYTELLING? WTF?

What is storytelling really about?

Storytelling is a fancy word that describes our love for identifying with something and feeling part of a story. We connect with that story, and that story becomes your product/service/brand. How do you do this effectively? Where's the data? How can you recognize a good storyteller?

Just because "story" is in the word "storytelling" doesn't mean your CEO should read a bedtime story to their biggest client (though it might help in some cases). Instead, it's about understanding that you're not selling (marketing, if you will) a product but a solution. Our brain's comfort zone is storytelling. Take the 'Memory Palace' technique for improving memory; it essentially involves scattering the words you want to remember in 'rooms' you've created in your imagination. You can then walk through the 'palace' to find the words you want to remember. Simplified, the idea is straightforward—

you build a story from a list of words because that's how our brain works best.

So, how do you do it best?

Audiences.

You should spend most of your time and effort identifying, analyzing, and getting to know your audience inside and out. Once you deeply understand your audience, you'll "discover" the most suitable and impactful story for them. It's like magic. In-depth and wide-ranging research into your audience will reveal so much that everything that comes after will be easy. When you truly know who you're talking to, you also know what hurts them, what they worry about, what to say, how to say it, when to say it, and where to say it. That's the art of storytelling in a nutshell.

It's not just words.

A good story isn't just a string of words and sentences. It's about creating an overall experience. Visuals, sounds, and emotions are used to paint a vivid picture in your audience's mind. Like a good book, the picture forms in the reader's head. The best example is Apple's "Think Different" campaign. They didn't mention product features at all, but viewers were left with so many emotions that directly connected them, in a good way, to the product and sparked a desire to buy.

It's not just for big brands.

Storytelling isn't just a method for big, wealthy brands. Even small businesses have enough stories to tell. True, the production and intensity might not match, but even storytelling done over time (due to budget constraints or current sales focus) still allows you to tell a story and connect with your audience. It will take longer, so don't give up.

The power of data in storytelling: Trust the data.

Data plays a critical role in effective storytelling. From deeply understanding your audience's behavior patterns and trends to evaluating the impact of campaigns and messages, statistical research aids decision-making. In the sea of data, you can always find a behavioral pattern or key insight. It's not just about what you see in the data but also what's missing from it. Good data also helps you understand which story will resonate emotionally with your audience and which story will drive identification and a desire to act.

How to spot a good storyteller (and avoid a bad one):

- **Good storytellers don't come to you with answers—they come with questions.** The first question should always be, "Who is your audience?"

- **The second question should be, "Where's the data?"** You can't make decisions based on what *seems* right. You need data for analysis before making decisions. An essential part of the process is knowing which questions to ask to obtain useful data for decision-making.
- **Good storytellers seek points where the audience identifies with your product/service/brand without clichés.** The story's details create the right connection, not the frame.

Remember, the best stories are real, captivating, and leave a lasting impression. So, start creating your stories and watch your brand flourish!

19

FIND YOUR BOREDOM. IT'S CREATIVE

I might be old (over 50 is the new 30, right?), but people are getting obsessed with automation not only at work but even in their private lives, allowing them to have more time to do something else, or in other words – getting even busier.

And that's sad.

I see so many posts and a growing number of groups centered around automation and productivity. Turning your life into a semi-robotic process might give you comfort that you are constantly active, but it leaves creativity outside, and that's even more saddening. Questions like "How can I be more creative?" start popping up.

There's no app for being creative, and it definitely won't show up when your day is so full of projects, meetings, and other "things to do".

People wake up with an app that scrutinizes their sleep and check it out. Then, an app that tells them what to eat, wear, and how to breathe. Then, an app that helps them concentrate while automating their workplace and life, and whatnot.

The 'HOW' to live better has sadly turned into the WHY.

It seems that everybody is afraid of some off-time. Like they might die if they find a boring moment or, god forbid, a project-free few hours.

Well, let me tell you this: you WILL die if you keep up this lifestyle.

Give yourself the gift of boredom. Let your mind reach that point where you have no practical thought about what you need to organize, what you need to do, who you need to speak to, etc. Let your mind drift into emptiness.

There it is, see it?

That little sparkle at the end is called creativity. Now say it with me: Cre-a-tivity.

That is what's going to keep you going.

Find Your Pause

That moment in the rush of things that lets your mind drift. That's when you're going to find that 'out-of-the-box thinking', that creative solution to that annoying problem at work or in your home.

We each have our different kind of pause, but we all need one.

Try This:

Stop at the corner of the street and look at passers-by. Just look. Let their stories come to mind. See how it fills your brain with thoughts, solutions, and color. Breathe in. Look at more people, cars, kids, old people, police officers. Smile.

It sounds "new age", but it's the one thing that humans have abandoned over the years and, with all the technological advances and screens, have really been missing.

You could already have a pause of your own and just haven't identified it as one, so take some time to put your finger on it and give it some more time.

Find - your - pause.

20

CONTENT IS NOT JUST WRITING!

I've been talking to some potential clients, and often times I've been asked, as a content person, about writing. Yes, I, and other content people, write; we write articles, marketing materials, user manuals, and other text-related stuff, but that is only the tip of the iceberg.

Content is Not Just About Writing

Writing is one of many options that arise from content strategy and analysis. In some cases, I would see a need for writing; in other cases, writing would not be necessary. Writing is a result or an option when tackling a case. When I say that I'm a content guy, it doesn't mean that all I do is write.

Content is all about giving or receiving information. It's not a conversation; it's the bulk data that flows in one direction. When it's good content, the data flow is used, consumed, understood, and accepted, leading to the target stated at the beginning (sales, awareness, or anything else).

That data could be a user manual or an article with tips about keeping your diapers white, but it could also be a slogan, a logo, a picture, a TV ad, a statue, a painting on a sidewalk, a billboard sign, T-shirts on a bunch of college kids, etc.

The Content Package

I might be stepping on some toes by saying so, but content is a package that connects your brand/product/service to the customer (or potential customer). It includes advertising, marketing tools, and writing if needed.

The end user of your content needs to find a use for that content. If the content is not aimed, directed, or delivered correctly, you miss out on a customer. The end user must "get" something from your content. It is the added value that could make that customer a happy one, which in turn usually means a returning one.

The Role of a Good Content Person

A good content person does advertising, marketing, point of sale (POS), analytics, research, testing, and whatnot. If, after all that, they believe writing is needed, then they write. We do not "do writing" on our first meeting :-)

If all a client wants is writing (user manuals, technical

writing, or SEO), then they can freelance one of many companies that do exactly that. But to get to that point, a client needs to know that all they need is writing. A good content person is what is needed at the beginning in order to assess the whole picture; in-house or outsourced is not the issue at hand.

21

IT'S PRESENTATION TIME. TIPS TO MAKE IT WORK!

The main goal of any presentation is simple: deliver your key message to the right audience. But that's easier said than done. A good presentation must convince your audience to trust you, understand your idea, and spark action, all while keeping them engaged.

Here are essential tips for crafting a winning presentation:

- Know Your Audience

Tailor your presentation to fit your audience. Whether you're pitching to investors, customers, or journalists, understanding who you're speaking to is crucial. Each audience will require a different approach.

- Use Psychology

Utilize the "recency effect," meaning people remember what they hear last. Repetition also helps anchor key points. Structure your presentation with this in mind.

- Tell a Story

Stories are memorable. Build your presentation around a narrative that highlights the problem, your solution, and the results. A compelling story is 22 times more memorable than mere facts.

- Keep Text Minimal

Use bullet points and avoid reading directly from the slides. Your slides should support what you're saying, not mirror it. Headings should guide you and your audience.

- Use Visuals Wisely

Visual aids should enhance, not overshadow, your message. Use high-quality images and avoid overloading slides with too much information.

- Consider Video

If appropriate, use calm, subtle videos as backgrounds, but avoid distracting movements or text-heavy clips.

- Follow the 10/20/30 Rule

Guy Kawasaki's 10/20/30 rule suggests 10 slides, a 20-minute presentation, and no fonts smaller than size 30. It ensures focus and clarity.

- Engage the Audience

Ask relevant questions that help you build your message. Interaction keeps the audience engaged and avoids pointless questions.

- Build Credibility

Support your message with research, quotes, and data. Credibility is key, but don't exaggerate. Be truthful and realistic about outcomes.

- Practice Makes Perfect

Structure your presentation first, then build out the content for each slide. After that, the most important step is to practice—repeatedly.

- Leave a Lasting Impression

Your presentation is about creating a memorable experience, so always focus on what you want your audience to take away.

22

DEATH TO THE SOCIAL MEDIA 'NICE TO HAVE' PAGE

If you're not a brand that can afford a team of social media people, then you have two choices: outsourcing (for big companies) and in-house management.

The Case Against Outsourcing

I do not like outsourcing when it comes to my brand, even if it's a small one. My brand is my income. Social media today is the first interaction your brand will have with a potential customer. If you screw it up, you lose a customer.

When your social media is outsourced, it is much easier to screw it up, as the only interest that outsourcing firms have is money. You and your team have more invested in the brand than just money, so what you need to do is wake up, stop holding on to a social media outlet simply because it is nice to have, and start building your social brand.

The Importance of First Impressions

When you meet somebody new, it takes you seconds to put him or her in a category in your head, and that's exactly what happens when somebody meets a new brand.

When you're a multimillion-dollar worldwide brand, it's easier to do everything right and everything wrong. It will be much harder to screw up your brand just by having a crappy social media outlet.

So, if you're not a mega-brand, start using it. In time you will see that it will increase your income and be almost a solo player in building a good reputation.

Building an In-House Team

Get someone in-house. Get them passionate about your brand. Yes, sometimes you must pay more to get someone passionate about an unknown brand. And get that in-house team or person to know every bit of what happens in your company. Everything.

Let them be part of your company and find out how much time it takes Phil from accounting to pay Sam from design. Social media people are the representatives of your brand. They are the new faces of you. So they need to know how you work.

When they have enough info, they will know how to answer best to any questions or complaints. When customers get good answers, they tend to lose their hostility towards your brand.

Creating Added Value

A good social media team or person would know how to get added value content from Bill, the truck driver and from Steve, the geeky technician. Customers who get added-value content tend to like your brand more.

A good social media team or person will know how to turn a potential customer into your very own ambassador, praising your brand for being there when they needed you. And yes, answering an online question in less than an hour is a good start.

In-House vs. Outsourcing

I'm not telling you to get rid of your outsourced team. I mean, I am, but only if you can afford an in-house one. What I want to emphasize here is that social media stopped being a 'nice to have' project a long time ago. You should invest in a good social media team or person, in-house or outsourced.

23

PROVOCATION AND ITS IMPACT ON THE MESSAGE (WITH A SAD CONCLUSION)

Simplifying Messages and Stirring Controversy

In the heat of election season, messages often get oversimplified. Instead of each side promoting its own offerings, it's easier to attack the opponent. Why discuss your vision when you can simply bash the competition?

Provocation is Easier

The quickest way to generate noise isn't by saying what you're good at, but by saying that one candidate's spouse doesn't vaccinate their children. In the commercial sector, the equivalent is to announce a new price cut for a pair of pants by parading young girls in swimsuits. Benetton (remember them?) used a picture of an AIDS patient moments before death.

Make Some Noise

When you create provocation, you're stirring trouble. But the question is, does the noise serve the company's or politician's goals or not? That is what ultimately matters. Creating provocation and noise for the sake of provocation and noise means you need to see your therapist.

So, is any publicity good publicity?

The Problem

Provocation can create noise quickly and reach almost everyone, like wildfire. But the downside is that the noise often revolves around the provocation itself rather than the intended message. The provocation BECOMES the message, and the original message gets lost.

When someone wants to protest the use of fossil fuels and does so by burning a car in the middle of the road, that's what people will hear, and the conversation will be set around the action itself and not the cause for it. When you see a campaign that has an obvious provocation, it gets the campaign in the news—great PR, but you can be sure that statistically, people don't remember what the company wanted to say, and the brand gets a negative connotation attached to it. It's like a fight that lasts for years and no one remembers what it started.

The Conclusion

Provocation creates noise, but if you use it, don't try to convey any crucial message alongside it because that message will be drowned out, and you (and your audience) will be left with the provocation and the feelings it created instead of the message. So think hard if provocation is the way you want to go.

SECTION 5: TEAM BUILDING AND LEADERSHIP

24

WHAT I LEARNED ABOUT TEAMWORK DURING A 5-DAY HIKE IN THE ALPS

It may sound funny to some, but every team should be comprised of various human being characteristics, just like your group of friends. Taking your best employees and replicating them will be a mistake that will cause tension, unhealthy competition, blaming, and lying.

While hiking the TMB (Trail Du Mont Blanc) with my group of friends, one could see the differences that built an amazing trip. And yes, you CAN compare it to any workplace. It's not rocket science, but it also isn't a shoe factory. The basis of creating a workplace environment for a group of people to become an efficient team is transparency and trust, and every team member should have the same goals in their mind. On top of that, the manager should be a leader. Many can manage, but leading is much more than that.

We're talking about building a team. So when you are

searching for new members for your team, you should not only think about the position skills but also about the team skills. These characteristics are, of course, on top of handling the responsibilities of their job.

Just like in my group of friends, here are some characteristics you should search for in new candidates. It's not a must, of course; it all depends on team size and needs, but these are some examples of the types of employees you would need to create an amazing teamwork environment:

1. **The Navigator** - The informal leader of the team. This person has it in them to find the best process to work with. They will be the one who offers ideas and direction to the manager about best practices, new processes, and more. Usually, weak managers fear these types of employees, but you shouldn't. If the manager IS a leader, these people will be their right hand.
2. **The Nerd (in a good way)** - They are the curious ones. They like to see what's new in the market, what competitors do, how technology is moving, and how the future may look for the company or department. This person loves knowledge and loves to spread information around.
3. **The Fast & Strong** - This is the person who keeps working even when all others have had enough for the day. They complete tasks faster than others and come back to help others.

4. **The Funny** - These people make the ride fun. They keep the workplace in a positive atmosphere and brighten everybody's day. They turn any task into an energetic and fun time together. They are funny but also trustworthy.
5. **The Glue** - The person who works at keeping the team together. They smooth things out; they talk... really talk to everybody about life, happiness, etc. They keep the team together.
6. **The Wise** - This is the person with more experience than others. They have insightful inputs that can make working much easier. They put things into the correct perspective and calm things down.
7. **The Friend** - They are everybody's shoulder to cry on. Trustworthy and the pillar of the team.

Building the Ideal Team

The ideal team isn't composed of identical members but a mix of individuals who complement each other's strengths and weaknesses. This variety fosters a dynamic environment where creativity, support, and efficiency thrive. As a leader, recognizing and nurturing these roles within your team can lead to a more harmonious and productive workplace.

By assembling a team with these diverse characteristics, you can create a work environment that is not only effective but also enjoyable. Each member brings their unique strengths, and together, they form a cohesive unit that can tackle challenges and achieve goals with greater synergy and success.

25

FIVE THINGS ABOUT TEAMBUILDING

See Your Team as a Unit

When building a marketing or content team, it's essential to see your existing team as a single unit rather than a group of individuals. Leading them as a unit means guiding them toward a common goal. As a leader, your role is to steer the team toward that goal, not just manage them to "do their jobs." That's the job of managers, not leaders. ;-)

Google's Project Aristotle provides a compelling example of this concept. Through research, they discovered that psychological safety was the top factor for high-performing teams. When teams operate as a unit, members feel safe expressing their ideas and concerns, which leads to innovation and improved collaboration. Similarly, Apple's marketing team doesn't work in isolation. Instead, they collaborate closely with product design, engineering, and customer service, ensuring that the entire company operates as a cohesive unit to deliver a unified message.

Continuously Improve the Unit

Once your team functions as a cohesive unit, your role is to help them get better and achieve goals. This involves identifying what will make the team more effective and uncovering any hindrances or missing elements. Netflix's culture of "Freedom and Responsibility" embodies this principle. The company empowers teams to take risks and make decisions while encouraging constant feedback, which helps identify missing components and areas of improvement. Similarly, under Satya Nadella, Microsoft shifted to a growth mindset culture, encouraging teams to learn from their failures and always strive for better results. Nadella fostered a sense of purpose and empowered teams to experiment and share knowledge.

Avoid Duplicating Your Top Performers

A common mistake is replicating top-performing team members. If you duplicate what's already there, no matter how good it is, you're simply maintaining the status quo. While maintaining the status quo is useful in the short term, it's tough to grow and expand. At Pixar, this idea has been embraced fully. Their creative team includes professionals from diverse backgrounds, ensuring fresh perspectives and unique storytelling. They hire for a range of skills rather than replicating existing roles. Spotify's approach to cross-functional squads also illustrates this point well. They focus on combining unique skills from engineers, marketers, and designers to create innovative solutions rather than duplicating roles.

Strive for Improvement and Growth

The goal is to keep improving because every quarter and year, goals and objectives increase. The team needs to meet those growing expectations. Duplicating the current team makes this difficult. New team members should be seen as adding value and enhancing the unit. Identify the additional talent needed to scale your team effectively. Amazon's Leadership Principles emphasize hiring talent that adds value to the team and drives continuous improvement. Leaders focus on raising the bar with each new hire. HubSpot's Culture Code encourages employees to continuously learn and experiment. They're urged to share knowledge and support one another, ensuring that the team is always improving.

Tips for Building a Stronger Team

1. **Isolate Desired Traits:** Identify the traits you need in this "independent unit." Do you need speed? Creativity? Impeccable organization? Data

literacy? List all the needs and requirements. Dropbox's marketing team recognized the need for both data analysis skills and creativity. They hired data scientists to complement their creative marketers and create data-driven campaigns.

2. **Analyze Your Existing Team:** Look at your current team. What traits do they have, and where do they need strengthening? This should guide HR in finding the right candidate. Salesforce regularly reviews the strengths and weaknesses of its marketing team to identify skill gaps. They then work with HR to hire candidates who fill those gaps, ensuring the team is well-rounded.
3. **Build a Learning Culture:** Foster a culture where continuous learning is valued. Encourage team members to take courses, attend workshops, and share their knowledge with others. LinkedIn offers employees access to LinkedIn Learning, where they can take courses and improve their skills. They're also encouraged to share what they've learned with their teams.
4. **Encourage Collaboration:** Promote cross-functional collaboration. Encourage team members to work with different departments to gain new perspectives and share expertise. Atlassian's "ShipIt Days" encourage employees from different departments to collaborate on

innovative projects for 24 hours. This promotes teamwork, creativity, and knowledge sharing.

5. **Celebrate Success:** Recognize and celebrate team achievements. This reinforces positive behavior and motivates the team to continue improving. Adobe's "Team Recognition" program allows employees to nominate teams for exceptional performance. Winning teams receive rewards and recognition at company-wide meetings.

26

FROM MANPOWER TO CUSTOMER SUCCESS TO HR BRANDING – CHANGING THE GAME

In a nutshell, I'm storytelling the industry's approach to human beings as a way to show that if you want change, one that is considered a risk, you first need to say it out loud, and the reality will follow.

Not long ago, and unfortunately in some companies today, you can still see 'Manpower manager' on someone's office door. The word 'manpower' embodies everything that was and is wrong in business. First, it's a gender thing, but let's put that aside.

It's the whole concept that industry relies on power. I mean, once the industry did rely on power, but it also relied on women; during WWII, women were hired to work in the steel industry and other factories while their husbands fought in Europe or in the Pacific. It was all for the cause.

As time went by and high technology was born, new jobs emerged and brought with them the concept of the human being who is the employee. The title 'Manpower manager' was replaced with a plethora of names and titles, all trying to show off how they believe that putting the human in the center was the solution for everything: Human Resources Manager, People Manager, and more. Of course, it took some time to reach a point that actually put the human in the center (or close to it). It went a bit too far with several Silicon Valley companies, making the employee so central that they couldn't leave. I mean, leave at the end of a working day. They were kept on and on and on into the night, or as we all know it – the golden cage idea.

More time went by, and suddenly, a new trend of putting humans in the center emerged – but this time, the human in the center was the customer and new jobs emerged, replacing the ol' account manager. You're not managing an account, but the people or company behind it. So, customer manager was born, which evolved into customer success, because the customers' success is our success.

While these two concepts lived separately, in the past couple of years, they merged into a new idea of how to run a successful business. But today, the spotlight goes three ways:

a. **Customer/Client**

b. **Employee**

c. **HR Brand Communications**

The new title – HR Brand Communications Manager, was born out of the need to highlight the company as a great company to work for and move forward with. It's basically trying to win the hearts of amazing employees elsewhere to come work for us. It puts the customer and employee in the middle with an overlapping, which is the company.

This progress in human-centric approaches is a concept in motion. Bringing us to this point was a lot of hard work and daring on the side of large companies. Unfortunately, they started shifting in thought only when competition was knocking on their doors. But still, they seeded the idea, and reality followed.

I'll end with the famous quote from *Field of Dreams*: "If you build it, he will come." If you want something to change drastically – start by stating it out loud. Yes, it could mean you'd be considered out of your mind, but only the great ones are!

27

IS THE CMO ROLE DISAPPEARING? NOT AT ALL

I recently read about another established company that decided to eliminate the CMO role from its organizational structure. If this were TikTok, that trend wouldn't have survived 2019. But even before that, companies like UPS, Etsy, McDonald's, Johnson & Johnson, Uber, and others chose to drop the CMO role. The reason? The role is "empty" because the "new world" of marketing already exists in other positions like strategy, content, data, sales, etc. So there's no need for such a role. "It shows we're moving forward." But that's not the case.

So, if you're a CMO, there's no need to worry.

What really happened is that, in recent years, top brands —or rather, the captains of these brands—realized they must change the direction of the giant ship they command or risk crashing into the growing iceberg ahead.

I deliberately wrote "captains" because the image that springs to mind when hearing that term fits perfectly: a collection of "older" CEOs, set in their ways, who still call the internet "new media." Well, you get the idea. :-)

They finally woke up. They realized, albeit a bit too late, that traditional marketing as they knew it had evolved and disappeared. So, what do rigid people do, those who don't want to rock the ship too much and create waves? Instead of steering the ship away from the iceberg, they just slowed down the pace towards it.

They continue to work in the old-fashioned, entrenched way, simply without a marketing person. Yes, other parts of the company overlap with various marketing roles, but when the fundamental approach hasn't changed, these overlapping roles aren't managed cohesively. This creates poor communication between the different departments. And what happens when communication is lacking? Mistakes are made, opportunities are missed, more money is wasted, and most importantly—the company's consistency starts to crumble. Messages aren't aligned, coordination is missing, and so on.

Some of these companies, like McDonald's, quickly realized their mistake and reinstated the CMO with a newly defined role. Thank goodness.

Today's Marketer: A Jack-of-All-Trades

Today's marketer must be a "jack-of-all-trades": a strategist, creative, data expert, content creator, audience analyzer, sales-oriented, a bit of a prophet, doctor, psychologist, and so forth. Today's marketer, even a few years back, is a bottleneck between what's happening within the company and how it's communicated externally, whether it's in sales, branding, investment, or strategic initiatives.

Before Canceling the Role, Understand the Changes

So, before you consider canceling a role, senior or not, understand the changes that have occurred. What made this role feel "empty"? Then, adapt the entire environment, not just that specific position. In your day-to-day as well, if something doesn't work, it doesn't mean that specific thing failed. You need to analyze all the data, not just its isolated stats.

For instance, if a campaign's CTR isn't performing well, it doesn't mean the text or image isn't good. There are many other factors that, together, reveal a bigger picture, including unmeasurable scenarios like a wedding that no one attends because there's a World Cup final at the same time. That's data you just can't measure.

SECTION 6: ADVANCED MARKETING STRATEGIES AND INSIGHTS

28

SOMETIMES WE NEED TO REMIND BUSINESSES WHAT SOCIAL MEDIA IS ALL ABOUT

Heads_up: A Semi-Philosophical Rant About Businesses and Social Media

The Blurb:

Two basic topics most businesses forget after some time:

a) Social media is not simply 'another media outlet' to advertise upon.

b) Your brand's social media behavior reflects directly on your brand.

Death to the Message, Long Live the Conversation

Yes, yes, I know... this stuff is sooooo 2008, yet for some reason, it seems as if it needs to be reminded again and again, as brands and companies tend to lose track after some time.

In the past year or so, I have seen brands and marketers bury themselves in analytics. They look for new candidates who swim in the analytical world. They invest in analytical software and services. They do all this while forgetting, or putting aside, the one thing social media is based upon—content. Analytics are important, of course, but you first need to reach a point where your marketing is worth analyzing. The biggest mistake is beginning a brand's life with analytics instead of building a strong community.

There are still many SMBs who tend to take the shortcut or, unfortunately, have been told to take the shortcut by 'social media companies'. Mistakenly, they refer to social media and community pages as simply another ad space; "summer sale," they cry out. But they do not care what happens right after putting up that beautifully designed visual post.

The old-fashioned silver bullet style advertising, where a message would be conveyed to the public like it was the king's orders, is gone. It is still a viable way of advertising, but you need to have a strong community to allow yourself to do so. It can't be on a regular basis.

The "Old Ways"

The "old ways" have been understood by the "masses". People can now tell when they are being advertised. People also understand what social media is all about, and being a printed ad with color and movement is not it.

When people are being talked to as a mass, like "normal" ads do, they get offended. Human beings want to talk. When they log on to a social platform, they expect it to be social. Any other type of communication is insulting.

So when SMBs use social media simply as a media outlet to tell the world about themselves, they lose money. By "lose money," I mean that they lose credibility, loyalty, potential future purchases, and opportunities for sales.

"Come visit us, we're on sale" is a message. If it's at the end of a conversation, that's okay, but if it's on a regular basis—then you're doing it wrong.

When people comment on a friend's photo, the friend comments back. Then another friend comments, and another, and you each comment and re-comment. That is a social activity. People expect that from anyone who is on a social platform, especially from a brand they like and want to find out more about. They would not expect that when being on the company website or blog. But when on social media, they expect their favorite brand to be humanized.

You Are What Your Social Behavior Says You Are

Another change in brand-human contact which came upon us in recent years, is the fact that people see the social platform of a brand as THE BRAND. They will complain, ask questions, make suggestions, compliment, and get information from that social platform.

That brings me to the second problem, which is obviously

connected to the first; in order to save some money, SMBs will either get a kid to run their social media or give the whole thing to a third party. That's like building a company with the vision you had in your dreams and then giving it to some high school graduate to run.

Your brand's social platform page is THE BRAND. Whatever happens on your social page reflects directly on your brand. If your posts are full of bad grammar, that will reflect on your brand. If the page does not respond to posts, complaints, questions, and so on, it will reflect on your brand.

If all you do/allow is uploading messages on sales and pictures of products and how good you are, that will reflect on your brand (badly).

Think of yourself asking a police officer how to get from here to a certain address. Think of yourself asking the officer directly, but the officer looks over your head into the horizon and ignores you. What will you feel about police officers? Generalization is a basic human reaction. If you ignore your customers or potential customers, they will eventually ignore you.

So the social platform has a catch in it—the customer regards your social presence as your shop's showcase window, but on the other hand wants the interaction as if he was in the shop.

You must make the customer or potential customer feel exactly that; make him believe you are listening to him while trying to sell, while showing off. Mission impossible, isn't it?

Why Third-Party Companies Came In

That's why third-party companies came in—to take on the task of being the brand itself instead of you, so you could continue doing what you do best—make money. But that is also the Achilles heel of digital marketing; no third party can really do it as well as you. Showing off your brand needs a belief and loyalty that only insiders have. A third party can be close enough, depending on what marketing world your brand is from. And if the third company has good people and not college students doing it for the money until they graduate.

So, if you want your brand to make it out there, either you do social media yourself, or keep a good eye on the ones doing it for you.

29

ARTIFICIAL INTELLIGENCE: THE NEXT STEP OR WHAT COULD LEAD TO ITS END, AND PIZZA

Artificial intelligence (AI) has helped us all in our daily lives. Humanity is now facing a technology poised to create a significant shift in both work and leisure.

Is AI Really Creative?

People often argue that AI isn't creative and, therefore, it could never replace humans in most creative jobs. This can be debated. Here's why:

The saying "Great minds think alike" helps illustrate the point. Our creative ideas are based on things we've seen, experienced, or heard. After processing and analyzing this input, our subconscious helps build a creative thought in response to a current need. We like to think our ideas are original and emerge from our imaginative minds, but that's only partially true. If you think about it, the number of times an idea was created "out of nothing" is very, very small.

We're Artificial Intelligence, Too

AI analyzes big data, which includes creations, experiences, and sounds from the past (depending on the data provided) and the present. Thus, any product of AI is ultimately based on existing things. Does that sound familiar? That's pretty much how humans operate, too. We absorb, digest, sort, and file everything we experience, see, and hear. Most of it vanishes into our subconscious and becomes the building blocks of a new (or 'renewed') idea.

The Power of Brainstorming

During the COVID pandemic, when employees were sent to work from home, many people missed brainstorming with colleagues. "Bouncing off ideas" isn't just a phrase; it's an activity that sharpens people, improves work efficiency, and produces better results.

And Pizza? What's the Connection?

A good idea is like a pizza. Every mind adds its own toppings to ultimately create a delicious Italian masterpiece (yes, pizza is a delicious Italian masterpiece!). One brain adds the flour (but only type 00), another adds water (but mineral), and someone else provides the tomatoes (only the San Marzano variety). It's the collective brainstorming, the back-and-forth between minds, that leads us to the final pizza. No single brain contains all the experiences and knowledge to lead us to pizza. Even the most creative mind will produce limited and incomplete results if it's working alone.

So What Can Set Us Apart from AI?

Brainstorming remains the key differentiator. AI can provide the best flour, tomatoes, and even arrange a wonderful khachapuri, but it can't make pizza. Why? Because proper brainstorming constructs an idea that's as good as creating something out of nothing. A new idea is built from bits, pieces, fragments, and experiences from various minds.

The Next Step in AI

The next step in AI is to facilitate dialogue between AIs, which could bring them closer to human brainstorming. But it will never work because human brainstorming is based on broken data fragments, not whole ideas as we think of them when we're alone. In brainstorming, our ideas are broken into parts and thrown into the air, and a new idea is constructed from them. AI can't break ideas down. It can connect whole ideas, but it can't create a new idea from randomly broken parts. And that's where we win.

Healthy Group Dynamics

As a creative group, we will always be able to beat AI, both now and in the future. There's hope for us. But when it comes to teamwork at work (departments, for instance), that's where suspicion arises. The dynamic is crucial. If the dynamics aren't right, brainstorming won't work. Without communication, transparency, trust, and reliability within the group, you might as well pack up and go home. Without a shared goal, brainstorming fails.

The Importance of Leadership

What else does your department need to brainstorm effectively? A leader. Not a manager, but a leader. A leader who knows how to turn a group of people into a unit.

Back to AI

Yes, if we can't form properly functioning teams, AI will beat us. If there's no leader to facilitate proper brainstorming with the right group, we will lose. We need to work on group dynamics at work, and then human brainstorming will remain our ace card over AI.

30

THE RISE OF CONTENT LEADERS: A NEW ERA IN B2B MARKETING

I'm still young, but what should have happened 20 years ago is finally happening, slowly but surely, around the globe. I have witnessed and have been part of the evolution of marketing over the years, and recently, a new "force" has been rising. Content leaders are shifting from traditional content roles into top marketing positions. This trend is not just a coincidence but a logical transition as a response to the changing landscape of marketing, which is increasingly becoming a demand-generation realm.

This is the moment to remind you that "content professionals" does not mean "writers." Content is a huge world of outcomes in which 'writing' is only one part. The traditional marketing model, primarily focused on advertising, sales, and lead generation, is giving way to a more holistic approach. This new approach recognizes that the customer journey is not a linear path but a spider web of interactions and multiple stages that require a consistent and engaging strategy.

In the B2B world, you can see it even better. The buying process is often long and complex, involving many decision-makers and a significant amount of research. In this context, content is not just a way to attract attention but a critical tool for educating potential customers, building trust, and, finally, driving quality demand. Content then continues to be the main jumping board for keeping the potential customer and decision-makers interested, engaged, and informed.

This is why we are seeing more and more content professionals stepping into leadership roles within marketing departments. Content professionals bring a deep understanding of how to create content and use it to engage audiences, nurture leads, and convert prospects into customers.

But what does this mean for the future of marketing?

1. **Recognition of Content's Value:** Firstly, it signifies a broader recognition of the value of content within the business world. Content is no longer just an SEO tool or a "fill the website with words" service. It's a highly strategic position. It's about creating meaningful connections with customers,

providing value, and building relationships that lead to business growth.

2. **Shifting Skills and Competencies:** Secondly, it suggests a shift in the skills and competencies required for marketing leaders. The ability to understand and leverage data, create compelling narratives, and engage audiences across multiple channels is becoming increasingly important.
3. **Customer-Centric View:** Finally, it emphasizes the importance of a customer-centric view. Content leaders understand that the key to effective marketing is not just about pushing products or services but about understanding and addressing the needs and interests of the customer.

It's not "This is what my service can do"; it's more "This is how I can solve your problem, which is XYZ." So, next time you think about the next executive marketing position in your organization, look outside the box.

31

THIS IS HOW NOT TO BE BORING IN YOUR ONLINE ACTIVITIES

Forward planning and meticulous analysis are part of the cornerstones of successful marketing strategies. However, in our quest for future initiatives, let's not overlook the power of retrospective content analysis – a pivotal yet often neglected aspect.

It's universally acknowledged that digital marketers excel in strategic planning, with meticulously crafted plans for upcoming campaigns, content schedules, and promotional activities. Yet, it's equally crucial to conduct a retrospective analysis. This means pausing and reflecting not just on the data gleaned from past endeavors but on the activities themselves.

Conducting a Retrospective Analysis

Take a moment to collect past activities, let's say, from the past three months, across a specific media channel into a comprehensive table (repeat this process for each medium). But don't just look at it! Take each campaign or advertisement and copy-paste it into a single document, allowing for a side-by-side-by-side comparison. Yes, it's a painstaking manual task, but the insights gained are invaluable.

Through this process, you'll likely discover recurring patterns – maybe same color schemes? Same text placements? or even repeated messaging? Moreover, you may identify instances where certain activities, such as frequent discount promotions, have become overused, leading to diminished impact and brand fatigue.

Recognizing Overlooked Patterns

Don't worry! You're not alone in this. Immersed in day-to-day operations, it's easy to lose sight of the bigger picture. Furthermore, an over-reliance on data analytics can sometimes obscure qualitative aspects of marketing performance. In some cases, stagnation or decline in results may be directly attributed to this oversight.

Therefore, taking a moment for introspection and retrospection is not just advisable; it's imperative. It's an opportunity not only to evaluate past performance but also to gain valuable insights into how your brand is perceived in the marketplace. Armed with a comprehensive understanding of past endeavors, you can chart a more informed and innovative course forward.

The Power of Retrospective Analysis

What's particularly compelling about a retrospective approach is its inherent capacity for ongoing improvement. Every backward glance, whether it's three months or three years, offers fresh perspectives and opportunities for refinement.

While numbers undoubtedly provide valuable insights, they seldom tell the entire story. By starting to use a retrospective mindset at the end of each quarter, you can unlock a wealth of data that complements the metrics, ultimately leading to a more effective marketing strategy.

Practical Tips for Conducting Retrospective Analysis

1. **Gather Your Content:** Collect all your social media posts, ads, blogs, and other marketing materials from the past few months. Create a comprehensive table for easy comparison.
2. **Identify Patterns:** Look for recurring themes, color schemes, text placements, and messaging. Recognize what has been overused and what has worked well.
3. **Evaluate Engagement:** Assess the engagement levels of different types of content. Identify which

posts received the most likes, comments, and shares, and understand why.

4. **Feedback Analysis:** Review customer feedback and comments on your posts. This can provide insights into what your audience likes and dislikes about your content.
5. **Adjust Your Strategy:** Use the insights gained from your retrospective analysis to adjust your future content strategy. Focus on what works and experiment with new ideas to keep your audience engaged.

By implementing a retrospective approach, you can ensure that your marketing efforts remain fresh, engaging, and effective. Remember, continuous improvement is key to staying relevant in the ever-evolving world of digital marketing.

32

DEATH TO THE MESSAGE, LONG LIVE THE CONVERSATION!

Customer Retention: A Tough Job

Customer retention is no easy task. When it comes to TV companies, newspapers, and other subscription services, retention often boils down to calling the customer who wanted to cancel and trying to convince them to stay. Many companies choose the easy (and cheap) path of sending offers and discounts via mail, but this messaging method is no longer effective.

The Digital Age: A Game Changer

The digital age has fundamentally changed—or rather destroyed—the old methods and forced companies to rethink their perception of the customer. Or at least, that's what was supposed to happen.

The old method relied on companies controlling their

customers through messages, whether it was mail, email, or advertising deals and discounts. Essentially, they told customers, "You will shop on the days and times that I dictate." Under this method, customers waited for the big company to tell them when to come and what to buy. The company delivered the 'message' to the customer.

The Interactive Era: Customers Demand a Conversation

Companies were caught off guard when the digital age became interactive. Today, customers no longer wait to receive messages from the company. They demand, criticize, respond to, and complain about the company. Many companies didn't know, and sometimes still don't know, how to respond because they were never required to "listen" to their customers. Listen? Since when? And more importantly, why?

Up to this point, whenever companies wanted to know what the customer thought, they turned to survey companies, and even then, only to help brand leaders decide how to approach customers next time. They never needed to listen to the customer.

The Archaic 'Message' Method Is Dead

It doesn't exist anymore. What we have now (or should have) is a "conversation" between the company and the customer.

The Conversation Is the New Message

Companies find themselves in a situation where they have to invest just to talk to a customer—and they're not even selling anything. This situation is challenging for sales managers. They're used to closing deals after such conversations, but now they're told, "No! I don't want to buy; I just want to talk to you." In any telemarketing company, if the representative knows there won't be a sale, they'll end the conversation in seconds.

Not too long ago, a customer who wanted to "just talk" would receive a slammed-down phone. The absurd thing is that the customer wasn't offended but returned to their expected role—receiving the message and going shopping. Companies that failed to adapt saw sales decline.

So What Is a Conversation?

A conversation is a straightforward process, but not necessarily simple. There's a reactive conversation where the customer initiates, and the brand listens, answers, talks, listens again, and so forth. Unfortunately, this is how most brands operate. Then, there's a proactive conversation where the brand initiates the conversation to learn more about the customers and increase trust, loyalty, and other positive emotions toward the brand.

Brands Miss the Mark

Brands often see a proactive conversation as "cool" but fail to learn from what customers are saying.

Why Is a Conversation Necessary?

Recently, the customer has leveled up and no longer sits at home waiting for a message. They demand a conversation. The main, albeit unspoken, goal is to give the impression (false or not) that the brand listens to the customer, is trustworthy, genuine, and an expert in its field. As a result, customers feel it's worth investing a little extra to buy from them and stay loyal.

Creating a conversation should also create buzz around it. The brand's conversation with the customer must happen publicly so potential customers can see that you're a brand that talks and perhaps join the conversation. Even if the conversation is an attempt to respond to a genuine and painful complaint, if it's not public, it didn't happen. It will help the specific customer and their immediate circle but won't have a wider impact.

Avoid the Private Conversation Trap

Brands must avoid inviting the customer to a "private conversation." They need to understand that if the answer isn't satisfactory, the private conversation won't stay private. The conversation continues post-purchase. Customer retention is also undergoing a transformation from defense ("No, please don't cancel") to offense ("If you stay with us, you can bathe in a milk bath").

Many Companies Still Operate with a Sales Mindset

Every action is expected to result in a sale. If there's no sale, they believe the action wasn't worth taking. This outdated thinking, which includes a severe lack of long-term vision, is slowly sinking these companies. They reach a point where they can't afford to change their mindset because they're only focused on survival. The result? Layoffs, losses, and bankruptcy.

What Does a Conversation Include?

A conversation isn't just an exchange of words. It's a mindset that must be embedded at every level of the organization, from the secretary to the CEO. It's a method that includes both long-term and short-term sales and marketing strategies, hence the confusion. The basic opportunities to create a conversation include social media, blogs, public surveys, transparency in decision-making, open and searchable technical support information, direct mail, humility, and more.

Become an Expert in Your Field

I want to elaborate on the term "humility." Here's a general example to clarify what I mean. If you have a fashion brand, a modest conversation could involve a series of articles throughout the year focusing on a fashion show in Paris (one you're not participating in, of course). By showing your potential customers that you understand the fashion industry as a whole, your image as a fashion leader will grow, as will your brand and, eventually, your sales. And you never once mentioned your brand—the conversation was about fashion in general.

In Conclusion

Brand leaders must start shifting from outdated marketing and sales methods of delivering messages to creating conversations. You don't need to allocate the entire budget to this method; just start directing a small percentage and increase it over time. True, there won't be immediate results, but in the long term, these brands will avoid bitter failure and be perceived as more sociable, trustworthy, and valuable, making them worth the extra investment over competing brands.

33

EVERY PROJECT NEEDS PIT STOPS TO REASSESS AND REASSURE

There are several people who have the ability to think out of the box, be creative all the time, and come up with new ideas when needed and, of course, when no one asks them to. Even these magnificent and enlightened people (did I say 'me'?) have their blind spots. Usually, these blind spots appear long after the idea has been given and the project is up and running. Everybody on the team is so in love with the idea and the implementation of it that they lose sight of the original goal or the changes that happened along the way.

Creative and marketing teams often follow an automatic working process, which isn't necessarily bad due to workload and lack of time. However, each marketing and creative team needs pit stops. Team managers must acknowledge the necessity of these pit stops and include them in their work plans.

A pit stop is a deliberate pause in the project, during

which team members take time off to clear their heads. This allows them to take a better look at the work done so far from a different angle and through a fresh perspective. The purpose is to ensure that the team and project haven't lost sight of the initial goals or missed changes that occurred along the way. The basic check is to see if the project is still aligned with its original goals. Other items on the pause checklist include customer views and needs, market changes, fresh ideas, and more. Have any of these changed during the course of the work?

Unfortunately, these project pauses are often neglected due to lack of time, lack of manpower, or even an excess of team member egos. This is why a new, fresh set of eyes needs to be introduced into the project.

These new eyes will join the team at critical pit stops during the project to provide an outsider's perspective. During a meeting with team members, the "visitor" will be given an update on the project's current status and progress. This visitor needs to be a very intelligent person who can analyze the situation and ask... stupid questions. Basic and seemingly stupid questions about goals, target audiences, customers, or budgets are often overlooked during the team's love affair with the project.

This person will play the devil's advocate, the customer's nagging mother, or whatever role is needed to make the team question their assumptions. The purpose of this questioning is to get the team out of their rut. The visitor needs to make the team rethink their project stages so they can make adjustments if needed or be reassured that they're on the right track. Even if everything is fine, the team needs to receive that feedback from both the outside and themselves several times during the project.

Using an outside pair of eyes is sometimes a simple solution that can save tens of thousands of dollars or more from going down the drain. An outside visitor saves time, money, and gives the team a much-needed focus slap. Try it.

www.ingramcontent.com/pod-product-compliance
Lightning Source LLC
LaVergne TN
LVHW091322150826
845673LV00006B/1734

* 9 7 9 8 8 9 5 6 9 9 3 7 9 *